The Ten Bridesmaids

Matthew 25:1-13

RETOLD BY MARY BERENDES • ILLUSTRATED BY ROBERT SQUIER

Distributed by The Child's World®
1980 Lookout Drive • Mankato, MN 56003-1705
800-599-READ • www.childsworld.com

ACKNOWLEDGMENTS
The Child's World®: Mary Berendes, Publishing Director
The Design Lab: Art Direction and Design
Red Line Editorial: Contributing Editor
Natalie Mortensen: Contributing Editor

LIBRARY OF CONGRESS CATALOGING-IN-PUBLICATION DATA
Berendes, Mary.
  The ten bridesmaids / by Mary Berendes; illustrated by Robert Squier.
      p. cm.
  ISBN 978-1-60954-395-2 (library reinforced: alk. paper)
  1. Ten virgins (Parable)—Juvenile literature. I. Squier, Robert. II. Title.
  BT378.T4B47 2011
  226.8'09505—dc22   2011004995

Printed in the United States of America in Mankato, Minnesota.
July 2011
PA02087

The parables of the Bible are simple, easy-to-remember stories that Jesus told. Even though the stories are simple, they have deeper meanings.

One day, a crowd gathered around Jesus. Many people asked questions about getting to Heaven. Jesus told them this story:

—◆—

Heaven is like ten bridesmaids at a wedding. Five of these bridesmaids were foolish. The other five were smart.

Before the wedding, the bride gave the ten bridesmaids a job. They were to wait outside the gate for the groom. He was traveling from far away, and was due to arrive soon—but no one knew the exact time.

The sun was beginning to set, so each bridesmaid took a lantern. The five foolish bridesmaids grabbed their

lanterns quickly and left. But the smart bridesmaids thought ahead! They brought extra oil for their lanterns.

The bridesmaids waited all evening for the groom. Darkness fell, but he still hadn't arrived. The maids had waited so long, the flames in their lanterns went out. Soon the bridesmaids fell fast asleep.

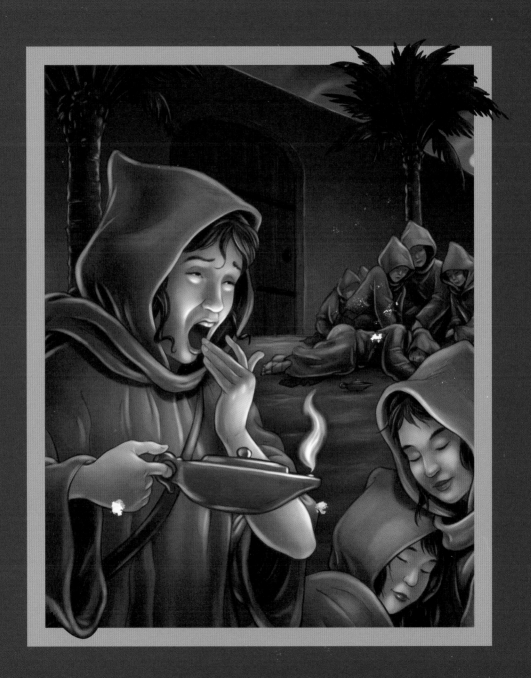

Hours later, someone shouted, "The groom is coming! Get ready to welcome him!" The ten bridesmaids woke up and reached to light their lanterns. But the foolish bridesmaids did not have any oil left! Their lanterns would not light.

They begged the smart
bridesmaids to give them
some oil.

"But if we give you some oil,"
said the smart bridesmaids,
"we won't have enough for
ourselves. You need to go and
buy some of your own."

The foolish bridesmaids hurried off to buy some oil. While they were gone, the groom arrived. The smart bridesmaids' lanterns were burning brightly. They welcomed the groom and walked with him into the house where the wedding was to be held. The door was then locked behind them.

When the foolish bridesmaids returned, they found that everyone else was at the wedding. They shouted and knocked at the locked door, but no one would let them in.

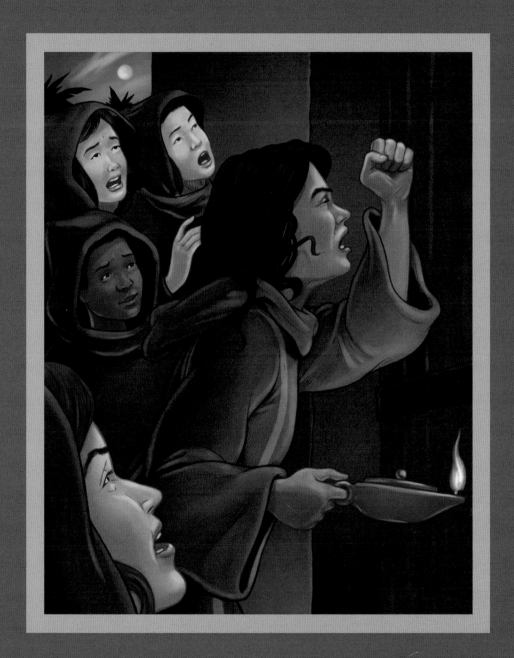

"Like the smart bridesmaids, you must always be prepared," said Jesus. "Every day, you must lead a kind, good life. You never know when it will be your time to enter the Kingdom of Heaven."

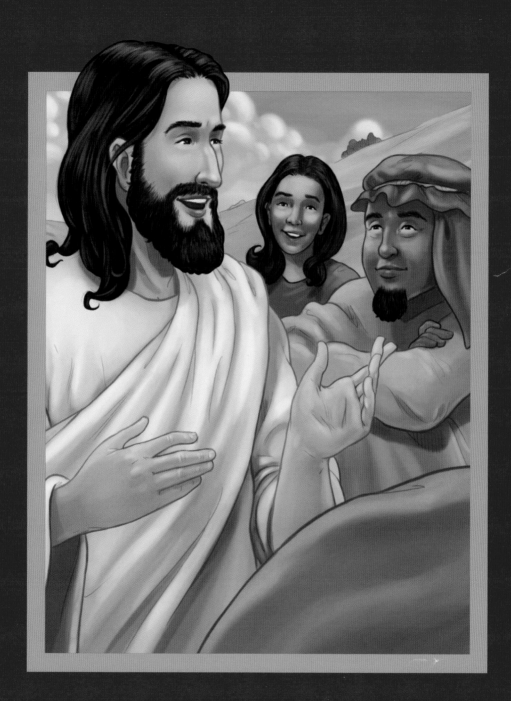

BEYOND THE STORY

The parable of the ten bridesmaids is a story Jesus told to help his followers understand that they were to always be prepared and ready because no one knows when it will be their time to enter the kingdom of heaven.

In the parable, Jesus uses bridesmaids to represent the children of God. The bridegroom represents Jesus and his return. All of the bridesmaids set out to welcome the groom. However, five of the bridesmaids were foolish. They did not want to take the time to make sure their lanterns had enough oil. They represent the people who always put off doing God's will until another time. They figure they will always have more time to make things right.

There were five wise bridesmaids in attendance as well. They realized that the night was long and they might need extra oil to ensure a warm and well-lit welcome for the bridegroom. They represent the children of God who know that thinking ahead and being prepared helps everything run smoothly. They know this is how we should live if we expect to be prepared for Jesus' return.

As the night wears on, they all fall asleep. Much later one of the servants alerts them that the bridegroom is coming. When the bridesmaids wake up, they realize that their lanterns have gone out. The wise bridesmaids are prepared and ready with the extra oil. The foolish bridesmaids realize their mistake, but it is too late. They rush off to buy oil as the wise bridesmaids welcome the bridegroom and escort him to the house where the wedding will take place. The house represents the kingdom of God. The locked doors are a reminder that if we put off correcting our relationship with God, we may not be ready for his return. As a result we will be left out of heaven.

The message Jesus was trying to get across was simple: We need to live our lives in such a way that we are always ready for his return.

Mary Berendes has authored dozens of books for children, including nature titles as well as books about countries and holidays. She loves to collect antique books and has some that are almost 200 years old. Mary lives in Minnesota.

Robert Squier has been drawing ever since he could hold a crayon. Today, instead of using crayons, he uses pencils, paint, and the computer. Robert lives in New Hampshire with his wife.